from various sources. Please consult a licensed professional before attempting any techniques outlined in this book.

By reading this document, the reader agrees that under no circumstances is the author responsible for any losses, direct or indirect, which are incurred as a result of the use of the information contained within this document, including, but not limited to, — errors, omissions, or inaccuracies.

TABLE OF CONTENTS

Chapter 1. Introduction 7

What Does This Book Cover? 7

What Does This Book Not Cover? 8

What is a Shock Collar? 8

What Terms Will We Be Using? 9

Can I Use An E-Collar on Any Dog? 10

Are They Expensive? 10

Why Are There So Many Rumors? 11

Summary 12

Chapter 2. Selecting the Right Collar 13

What Size? 13

What Range? 14

What About Levels? 15

What Does Your Dog Like to Do? 15

What's the Best One? 16

Chapter 3. Benefits and Risks of E-Collars 18

Are E-Collars Inhumane? 19

Are Correctly Used E-Collars Dangerous? 20

What About When Humans Test a Dog Shock Collar?
....20

What Happened in 1980? 22

SHOCK COLLAR DOG TRAINING GUIDE

HUMAN E-COLLAR TRAINING TIPS AND METHODS, EVERYTHING YOU NEED TO KNOW ABOUT REMOTE COLLAR TRAINING FOR DOGS

JACK E. GARRETSON

Do E-Collars Burn Dogs? 23

Isn't It Dog Abuse? 24

Do They Work? 24

Will My Dog Hate Me? 26

Chapter 4. Before Training 29

When Should I Start? 29

What Can I Use An E-Collar For? 32

What Should I Never Use An E-Collar For? 35

Do I Have to Use an E-Collar if I Own It? 37

Chapter 5. Things to Watch Out For While Using An E-Collar 40

Is Your Dog Aggressive? 41

Does Your Dog Hate Remotes? 42

Does Your Dog Function Without An E-Collar? 46

Can You Say, "Short Term?" 48

Is Your Dog a Nervous One? 49

Are You A Lazy Trainer? 51

Is the Setting Wrong? 53

Chapter 6. How to Train a Dog Using An E-Collar 57

What About the Introduction Phase? 58

What About the Moderate Phase? 63

What About the Final Phase? 66

Are You Ready for Your Pop Quiz? 67

Chapter 7. Common Questions and Answers 70

Is E-Collar Training Hard? 70

Can I Just Use an E-Collar? 70

What If Stuff Goes Bad? 71

What If I Can't Afford a Name Brand Collar? 72

Is My Dog a Good Fit for an E-Collar? 72

Why Can't I Use My Grandpa's Hunting E-Collar? 73

Is E-Collar Training Expensive? 73

Will People Hate Me? 74

Chapter 8. Conclusion 76

About The Author 78

Chapter 1. Introduction

Well, you did it. You made the great choice of buying this book. Of course, you could be reading someone else's copy, but no matter how you got here, you're now reading along. Great! You're here because you want to learn more about E-Collar Dog Training, which is basically the King Arthur of the dog training world: a powerful, legendary thing, but with enough myths thrown in to muddle up everything until you can't tell what's fact and what's fiction.

What Does This Book Cover?

Never to fear, complete stranger! I'll be taking you through everything you need to know about it. Right now, whether you know absolutely nothing about E-Collar Dog Training or if this is a topic you've already researched, you'll come out better for having read it. Here's how this is going to go: we'll start with this handy-dandy **introduction,** breeze on through to the **basics** from selecting a collar to using it, hop over to the some of the **less basic stuff** like what to do if your dog gets scared instead of learning, and we'll end up on **the big questions** that everyone wants to know. Spoiler alert—no, your dog will not be burned by it, no matter how many times Jerry from Reddit has insisted that he's found burn marks from a shock collar. In short, this book is designed to use as a **One Stop Shop for all things E-Collar.**

WHAT DOES THIS BOOK NOT COVER?

This book is supposed to help you with making an **unbiased, safe decision on shock collars.** This can be, depending on who you talk to, a pretty passionate topic. I'm sure you'll find people who praise shock collars like they fell out of the sky on a golden chariot. There are other people who think they're inhumane and cruel. There's a good side to both of these arguments, and I will be **presenting both sides of the debate.** My job is not to convince you to go buy one or to scare you away. My job is to give you the facts, and let you sort out what you want to do with them. Good? Good.

Without further ado, let's start off with the boiler plate information here. For those of you who are more experienced, feel free to hop onto the next section, but I'll be taking it slow for anyone who wants to follow along.

WHAT IS A SHOCK COLLAR?

Where better to start than with Mr. Obvious question here: **what is a shock collar?** Answer—a shock collar is a (you guessed it) a collar you put around your dog's neck like a regular collar. In most every way, it looks and functions like a normal collar, except it's got the ability to administer varying levels of an electric shock. They exist as a **dog training device.** You, if you were so inclined, could use them on other parts of the dog's body, but the primary place you'll see this is around a dog's throat in the style of a traditional collar.

I'll get into the particulars later in the book, but for now, this is the boiler plate definition.

WHAT TERMS WILL WE BE USING?

By and large, shock collars go by a ton of different names. For this book, I'll try to keep things simple and not use a lot of those colloquialisms and nicknames, but some of the common terms include **shockers, electronic collars, remote training collars, e-collars, electro collars, Zap collars,** and more. Is that a conclusive list? Oh, heavens no. You've probably heard variations that aren't listed here, but these are some of the more common phrases.

CAN I USE AN E-COLLAR ON ANY DOG?

Absolutely. **No matter what size dog you have, there's an e-collar for your fluffy friend.** You do need to make sure you get the **right collar,** which I'll get into more in the next chapter, but for now, yes, any dog can use one. I remember reading about one idiot who tried to (very unsuccessfully, I might add) use one on an undomesticated wolf, so I want to be perfectly clear: **use these on domestic pets.** You could try, I suppose, on other animals, but for all intents and purposes, these things are not meant for anything other than a domestic dog.

ARE THEY EXPENSIVE?

A very valid question. Counter question—are cars expensive? Well, it depends on the model. You could go out and buy a million dollar sportscar that could never get off the highway, or you could find a cheap old pickup that's thirty years old that could never get as fast as a sportscar but is virtually indestructible. In other words, **it depends.** Different models have different strengths and you can pick them based on what fits best for your current situation. But, overall, these are priced to be more affordable every day. In the beginning, they were pricey. Now, your average person could probably do just fine buying one.

WHY ARE THERE SO MANY RUMORS?

Before I actually did the research, I thought that e-collars were the worst possible thing for my dog. I love him so much. He's a bulldog named Bongo, and I'd be damned if I ever did anything to hurt him. From everything I seemed to hear, putting an e-collar on him would do nothing but hurt his pretty little wrinkly self. Of *course* I didn't want to buy one. I mean, they cause burns and shock and can kill your dog and they can't be used in the rain or it'll electrocute your furry friend and—yeah. Let me stop you right there, and tell you this: **these have so many rumors because they exist in the age of the internet and people like to come up with rumors.** It's really that simple. I'm not going to tell you that there isn't a legitimate side to the people who don't like them, and later in the book I'll show you the argument against e-collars, but for now, trust me— these things are made to help. The overwhelming majority of the rumors are just that—rumors.

SUMMARY

O-kay, so, you read through the introduction. Congrats! Do you have any questions? If you do, too bad! I'm a writer you've never met and will never see, so I can't hear your questions. That being said, if you are curious, I will do my absolute best to answer any potential questions in the upcoming chapters. Ready? Let's do it!

CHAPTER 2. SELECTING THE RIGHT COLLAR

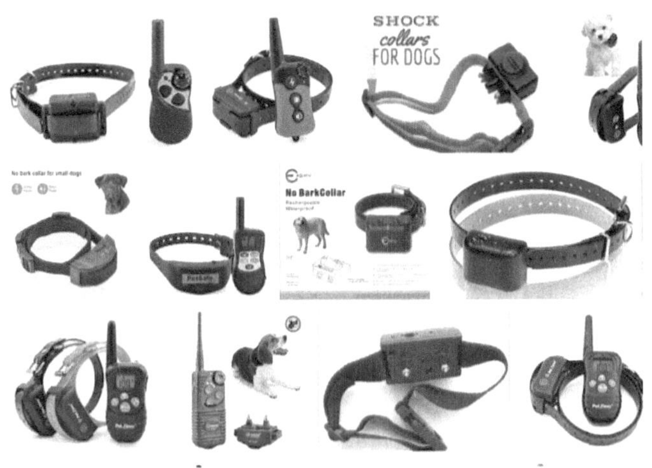

     Myth—there's only one kind of e-collar. It's this big, bulky apparatus you strap to your poor little Fifi and it's a one-size fits all, so of course you can't trust them because if they're meant for a Great Dane, then it's dangerous for your little chihuahua. Fact—**there's a ton of different options out there**, all of which are catered to your individual needs. Fact Number 2—I will help you figure out what you need for your individual needs, or at least make you aware of what options are out there. Here's a tip—**shop based on qualities.** Not all collars are made the same, and some will have traits that you like better than ever. Here are a few for you to pay attention to in particular.

What Size?

Like I said above, these collars vary enormously in size. **Get the one that fits your dog right now.** Yes, if you're training an adolescent dog, he or she will grow into a big strong dog, but for right now, don't buy an e-collar that he'll grow into. It's not meant to work that way, just like you wouldn't buy a regular collar that's too big. The reasons are about what you'd expect—too loose, and it might fall off or get caught on stuff, and too tight, it'll choke your beloved pet.

A brief note here—don't just wing it. You may know the approximate size of your dog's neck, but don't just wander into your local Petsmart and get something that looks basically the right size because it really does matter. **Measure your dog's neck size.**

What Range?

E-collars come with remotes. What this means is this—you see your dog chewing on your beloved Aunt May's porcelain piece of yard art. You don't want your dog to chew on your beloved Aunt May's porcelain piece of yard art, but you're too far away to do much. Luckily, you have a remote! Just activate the collar, and it will wireless transmit the message to the collar, which will, in turn, administer your preferred level of shock to the dog then and there. If you have a backyard that's a solid eight foot long, you don't need to have a collar with a massive distance. If you, on the other hand, use your dog for hunting, yes, you want a longer distance. Some of the models can get **up to a mile of distance.** To me, I can't imagine a lot of times where you'd need more than that, but they'll probably make a new one tomorrow that'll boast an even bigger rating.

WHAT ABOUT LEVELS?

Probably many of us have a very vivid image of something when we hear the words "electric shock." You're not tossing Fido into the electric chair. In the past, yes, e-collars didn't come with a lot of variation in how much of a shock that they can apply and that's where you get the image of e-collars being stiff and dangerous, but today **models come with tons of adjustments for stimulation levels.** Electricity is incredibly useful for all kinds of things, and many of the collars have options that aren't nearly as painful as owners might imagine. Remember, electricity is used for physical therapy on humans.

I'm not going to make a lot of principled stands on this book where I tell you what to do, but trust me— **buy only a collar with adjustable sensitivity settings.** The alternative is not something I'd even halfheartedly recommend. Start low, and if you need to, gradually increase levels in a safe manner.

What Does Your Dog Like to Do?

My sister's dog, a pom, is never more happy than lounging like a king inside on a couch. My dog, a bulldog of adorable proportions, would like nothing more than to stick his stubby nose into anything and everything outside. If I let him out and glance away for a quarter of a second, he will return covered in mud, grass, things I don't even recognize and that I'm not sure even originated on earth, and so much more. Why am I telling you this? Because my sister might want an e-collar that's *completely* different from mine, because I'd need one that's **waterproof and indestructible.** It'd be a mighty shame to lose your brand new collar because it got wet, but a word of warning—not all collars are equal. Just because something is technically waterproof doesn't mean it's the best fit for your needs. Go off ratings, advice, and buy from a licensed seller. Petsmart will not sell you something dangerous. That strange man who lives out of his van will, no matter how much he may insist that it's a completely safe one that's never been used.

What's the Best One?

Ah. The question. The thing everyone wants to know. I have bad news for you—there is not an answer to this. There's so many factors to consider. For some, the "best" might be the best bang for your buck. Others would rather have the top of the line. Others want just enough to get the job done. The list goes on. Blah, blah, blah. I couldn't in good faith tell you which one to buy, but as a rule of thumb, here's a few things to do when you're in the market for an e-collar:

Do You Know This Brand? If you know and trust the brand, the odds are that it's probably a good one. If it's something you've never heard of, it doesn't necessarily mean anything terrible, but keep your eyes peeled.

What About Reviews? Reviews are the lifeblood of this market. Believe it or not, people care a lot about their dogs and if something hurts their beloved pet, they'll shout it from the mountaintops. Do your research. If a collar has overwhelmingly terribly reviews, avoid it.

What? Maybe this whole thing seems overwhelming to you, and the only thing you can ask is "what?" Never to fear. You don't have to make this journey alone. If you feel uncomfortable making this choice or finding the right one, solicit someone who can. Many pet stores have knowledgeable employees who would be happy to find the right choice for you.

CHAPTER 3. BENEFITS AND RISKS OF E-COLLARS

Before I start this next chapter, look up "risks of E-Collars." Go ahead. I'll wait. You'll find a hundred different articles about why they're the worst thing ever, about how they're dangerous, inhumane, and should be illegal. You'll also find a hundred different articles on why the other hundred are completely wrong. In a way, it's kind of funny. The topics splits dog owners and trainers straight down the middle. So, which side should you choose?

How about this. Rather than diving into the "burn all e-collars" camp, or drinking the "e-collars are godsends" smoothie, both of which have their pros and cons, let's approach this like the rational adults we are. Here's the answer in short: **both sides are right, and both are wrong.** Extremists are very rarely correct. Usually, including this case, **the right answer is a middle ground.** This is a meaty chapter with lots to go through, so buckle up and let's go!

ARE E-COLLARS INHUMANE?

If you actually looked up the articles, you'll notice something very, very obvious right off the bat: **the articles are carefully written to twist your opinions by people who support either group strongly.** Supporters of e-collars use terms like "electronic training collars" and "electronic collar" while the opposition creates a very different image by using terms like "shock collars" and "shockers." The rest of the articles are just about as predictable as you might guess—one way or the other, hard line in the sand.

Spoiler alert—**I'm not going to take a stand on inhumane or not.** That's your call, 100%. Some people tend to believe that they're overwhelmingly inhumane. Others say they're perfectly humane. Pick a side, any side, or don't. It doesn't matter either way, because I'm not here to convince you on the morality of anything. I'm here to give you the facts.

ARE CORRECTLY USED E-COLLARS DANGEROUS?

Ah, here's a question I can actually help on. When I was first doing research, the very first post I found about e-collar training insisted that shock collars are dangerous. They also threw in the fact that the injuries were from "misused collar." They kind of tossed that in there on the side like nobody would notice. **If you misuse the collar, it isn't the collar's fault**. If you whack your friend in the face with your smartphone, you cannot now call your smartphone dangerous. You are, for using it like an idiot. Many of the articles that I found opposing e-collars were outdated on their information. Even one that came out days ago, one of the biggest articles, was **completely wrong about their information**. Example—they claim that "shock collars" max out at 400 yards. A quick Google search showed that multiple models are in the miles. I don't know where they got this information. Someone did not do their homework.

When used properly, **E-Collars are not dangerous.**

WHAT ABOUT WHEN HUMANS TEST A DOG SHOCK COLLAR?

I hate to sound like I'm bashing this article from above, but it's kind of a load of biased baloney. They even feature a video, **Humans Test a Dog Shock Collar,** which features a shirtless man wearing an e-collar and getting shocked at various levels, going up to 8 (which is max for this collar). It causes him obvious pain. Reader. I need you to understand this. Many modern e-collars go up to level 100, and experts recommend keeping them set for **levels 3-5 out of the 100.** This guy decided to put it on basically **level 100 out of level 100 (full strength).** That's stupid, and you are *never* supposed to go that high unless it's in extreme circumstances and most dogs learn with a few times at level 3-5. He starts at level 3 for his demo, which is level 37.5 on a normal collar—**ten times higher than is recommended**, and works his way up to full strength— which is **twenty to thirty-three times higher than you're supposed to.** No, duh, it hurts. Additionally, though the collar in question is a highly regarded one, many users only use the vibration aspect and find that even a level 1 shock isn't necessary. Catchy title, completely idiotic and not representative of what you're supposed to do at all. Being fit and working out is great for you, but do it thirty-three times higher than you're supposed to, and you'll have problems too.

Also, if you're curious, many dog training courses understand some people's hesitation about e-collars and ask their owners to use them on themselves at the recommended strength to alleviate their fears. It's not the terrifying electrocution that the myths would imply—unless you decide to do it at thirty three times higher than you're supposed to.

WHAT HAPPENED IN 1980?

Pop quiz—what does something in 1980 have to do with today's market for e-collars? Answer—nothing! One thing that you will hear often is the **US Center for Veterinary Medicine's** report back about 40 years ago, where one manufacturer was found to produce faulty collars that actually did hurt dogs (collars that were then promptly removed from the market). This one report is the basis for many of the fears and myths around e-collar training despite the fact that it's almost half a century old and shows that the government is active enough in this market to catch and ban any unsafe methods for the past 40 years. 40 years. Yes. Watch, I can do this too. Did you know that a bunch of models of cars in the 1980s had to be recalled because they were built unsafely? Therefore, I should not buy a new car today because they're dangerous! Gah. I hate to get on a rant here, but this argument is highly illogical. 40. Years. Of course, they're using the same technology that they did in the inception of e-collars, just like cars are the same, TVs are the same, phones are the same, laptops are the same, internet is the same... Sure. Check it out—Enron fell in 2001 with tons of legal tape around it like this one e-collar manufacturer 40 years ago, and twenty years more recently than this widely-touted source. What would the writer of this article surmise? Never get involved in a business.

Do E-Collars Burn Dogs?

They don't burn dogs. Sometimes, you can see what looks like an electrocution mark on your dog's neck. Some misinformed owners incorrectly make their own assumption of what caused it, when the truth is far more obvious than you might guess: **rotate your dog's collar several times a day (every four hours is recommended) or it will cause rubbing sores** where it connects with your dog. Owners that do not keep the collar in different places may notice these sores appear, but it's not from electricity. It's from the collar rubbing there for too long and is entirely preventable (especially if the collar is too tight). A few bad collars decades ago formed the idea, and people tend to fall to the least common denominator instead of realizing that many of the "problems" can be attributed to improper use. Also, bonus tip: if your dog happens to have a **nickel allergy,** they will not be a good fit for the more common contact points, as nickel is found in the stainless steel contact points.

Isn't It Dog Abuse?

Another hugely touted banner is that e-collars are dog abuse. It conjures up images of some dog abuser that loves torturing dogs by electrocuting them. There are a number of fallacies with this argument, namely that if someone was wicked and cruel enough to do that, they aren't going to shell out their money for something like this when an evil individual could abuse an animal with basically anything. These are terrible, terrible people, and should **never be confused with responsible dog owners wanting the best for their furry friend.**

Do They Work?

E-collars work well in almost every scenario. Even many individuals who see it as inhumane often admit that it is a very successful method for training dogs. Most dogs do not require more than a few corrections at very low levels (3-5 out of 100). Some will get it almost immediately with ridiculous success rates. The collars are designed to help them learn. Most (and the only ones I'd recommend) provide a warning beep before doing anything, giving the dog time to change their actions. Proper, diligent training with an e-collar mixed with other types of training, like treats (I'll get more into that later), can provide some of the best results. That being said, it's important to note that an e-collar should not be your first resort, because although they are successful, generally you will have more success with other training options, like positive reinforcement through treats. I'll get more into this later.

Also, a brief side note here—for those of you who have trained more than one dog or at least known someone who's trained more than two dogs, you know full well that every dog is different. One dog that I've trained, another Bulldog, was one of the smartest and most attentive dogs I've ever had the pleasure of seeing. Everything I did, he'd figure it out, from speaking to sitting to doing a wiggle dance. He was always extremely respectful, never pushed his boundaries, and blah blah blah. But he had a flaw. A really, really irritating flaw—he *hated* the leash. I mean, hated it. He was a perfect little doggo in every other way, but if you got that leash near him, he'd go ballistic, just a wrinkly little dollop of fury. I still have no idea why and I suspect I never will, but he was always thrilled to be near me, but if he even got the feeling that the leash might be nearby, he was horrified. For whatever reason, he just despised leash walking. Why did I tell you this? Is this Dog Training Story Hour? I told you this because it's a good example of how different methods work for different dogs. Some dogs may respond brilliantly to an e-collar and others might be like trying to push a boulder through the mud... with a rope. Few training exercises are as well established as the leash, but for such a candidate, it would probably be a good idea to try an e-collar.

WILL MY DOG HATE ME?

So, you bought yourself an e-collar, stuck it on ole' Spot, and now he knows not to bark at the mailman all the time. Congratulations! You're successful! But, as anyone with a heart and a pet knows, if your pet hates it so much that they now hate you, it's not worth it. I can't imagine causing pain to my dog. I feel terrible to even imagine that he'd ever hate me. I want our bond to be as clean and pure as possible, so this brings up an important question: does this actually have cons?

Fact—**Yes, e-collars do have drawbacks**. Even advocates for e-collars have to admit that this is not the dog training equivalent of those miracle pills that make you lose 25 pounds a month. Here are the big cons that need to be discussed.

--**No positive reinforcement**. Look, I hate it when my bulldog gets on visitors and slobbers all over them, but I hate negative reinforcement. I'd be much happier trying to teach him to continue to do the good things instead. If you're like me, you probably are in the same camp I am on that. This is a bit more of a personal thing.

--**Fear. Fear, bad. Fear, very bad**. Your dog should love you and trust you. Your dog should not think you're abusive and cruel. You do not want this. It's incredibly hard to repair a dog's trust (not to mention that a dog's fear can be very dangerous), and shock collars are relatively stupid. They're just machines, and they can't be sure what message your dog will pick up from the shocks. Let's say your dog barks at the mailman and you program the collar to shock her when she barks. A human would figure it out. A dog might now fear the mailman and think the mailman is hurting her. Then, your mail delivery person decides to deliver a package to your front door one day, and you've now got a problem. A dog will learn a lesson from any training technique, including e-collars. It just might not be the one you want them get from it. To us, to us humans, it might make perfect sense, but if your dog gets the wrong message, it can be bad for everyone involved.

--**Overcorrection**. Like I said before, these things are machines. They can make mistakes. Let me kick you a scenario here. You (hopefully) know that stealing is bad. If you don't, you steal something and get punished and you learn your lesson. But, then, without you stealing something, you still get punished for it and you don't understand anything. That's what happens when shock collars unintentionally or too often shock a pet, punishing them for something they didn't even do. This is especially true of automatic fence shocks and bark collars. If your dog pieces together that if he or she wanders too far out and get's disciplined, great. If your dog now just thinks the outside world is terrible and scary and mean and cruel and confusing, not great.

Chapter 4. Before Training

Woohoo! We made it past all the definitions and now is the time for action! You, even if you're a first-time dog owner, know that there is no easy answer for training dogs that works 100% of the time. There is no 2+2=4. You add 2+2 and you can sometimes get three and sometimes get five. Pets are, after all, living creatures, and though we love them, they aren't absolutely predictable all the time. There's a lot of variances and a lot of "if thens," like "if my dog likes belly rubs, then I can use them to help train." I won't lie to you. It can be a real pain to train a dog, especially when they chew up your Grandmother's beloved chair from Italy and somehow get slobber all over your clean clothes the *second* you turn your back. Yet, let me tell you, there's nothing more rewarding than successfully training a dog, and luckily for everyone, an e-collar can help! Before you throw your hands in the air and think it's hopeless, there are things that we do know— guidelines for training dogs using an e-collar. Here they are below!

WHEN SHOULD I START?

Let's get right into it. **You should not start with e-collars.** Many experts believe that it is better to train your dog without using negative reinforcement first, namely through treats, petting, and that kind of thing. If your dog works perfectly with this, good news! You don't need an e-collar. If your dog is a perfect example of obedience and is just getting everything you're saying and everything sailing along smoothly, it's best to not introduce an e-collar. That being said, if you take them to a different location, like a dog park, and all your lessons fly out the window and they proceed to forget every bit of training you ever gave them, it may be time to use an e-collar. Generally speaking though, the **"natural way"** of training is better and more likely to give you success—not to mention that it can alleviate any worries about safety.

Also, many experts insist that **no e-collar be used until very basic commands are understood,** namely your classic "sit," and "stay." Why? Because if your dog doesn't have a concept of it, they might not make the jump between barking endlessly and getting the negative discipline. They have to have some idea of what's going on for an e-collar to shine.

CONSULT A PROFESSIONAL

In an ideal world, everyone would know how to do everything, but in the world we currently live in, that's just not the case. **Before you use an e-collar,** be sure to **consult a professional.** This isn't for everyone. You, reader who's been training for the last thirty years, you probably don't need to do this. But, if you're a beginner or a relative beginner, I'd strongly recommend that you seek out a professional before embarking on e-collar training. Why? Well, for a number of reasons. Dogs are great, but dogs can be very, very different, and depending on the breed tendencies, history, learning styles, and more about your particular dog, you may need to change your plans. You don't want to spend tons of time fixing any mistakes you make right off the bat, because to an impressionable dog, especially a young and impressionable dog, your first lessons can be paramount and can be very difficult to fix later. Do it right the first time!

AGE

You may have just bought a puppy or you may have a ten year old, and obviously, you're going to need to approach those two very differently. But, here's the question you're going to need to make sure: **when is it safe to start e-collar training?** Well, I'd love to have an answer for you, and here's the best I can do: consult your veterinarian, because a lot of factors can go into if your dog is ready. Generally speaking, extremely small dogs and extremely young dogs are not good candidates for this as their smaller figures can be more susceptible to even smaller shocks. Most of the collars you would be interested in say the weight range that they're supposed to work with, but always go forward with care. The odds of something going wrong are very slim, but when your dog is involved, it's always better to make a thousand percent sure that you're being safe.

WHAT CAN I USE AN E-COLLAR FOR?

Basically everything. You name it, you can do it. Though of course the particulars vary from person to person, the most common uses are **to keep a dog from getting out of your yard and getting lost, to keep a dog from barking,** and other such things. By and large, they're to keep your dog from doing something incredibly frustrating or dangerous for them.

Many people **use an e-collar as a backup plan.** I remember reading one story about a young woman who was walking her dog in her neighborhood when he got away. Maybe the leash slipped out of her hand. Maybe it wasn't properly secured. Really, it doesn't matter how it happened, but all of a sudden, she's got her dog sprinting headlong towards the road and traffic. But, luckily for everyone involved, she had a backup plan. Her dog wore an e-collar that she'd barely used, finding that although he learned from the collar perfectly, she didn't need it and relied on other methods. Anyway, she hurriedly whipped out her remote that she carried for such occasions and activated the collar, bringing her dog to a safe stop before he, being the fluffy little idiot he probably was, charged headlong into traffic.

Another example is that of you ranchers or farmers out there, or really anyone with land. If you haven't run into it yet, the wilderness provides you with a whole wealth of unpredictable problems that can be extremely bad for your dog's health. Where I live is Rattlesnake Country, which, if you don't know that a rattlesnake is, they're snakes that tend to hide under cars, in tall grass, next to your porch, or really anywhere. Most importantly, they pack a serious punch, and a single bite to a dog can kill it, especially if it's on the facial region. They are to be taken very seriously, and where I live, they're everywhere. One month, we ran across twelve in a single month. Wherever you live, you might have similar problems. Whenever I'd take my dog out, I'd always worry about running across one. A rattlesnake will not charge. They're not aggressive, but they are more than happy to bite if pressured. Unfortunately, if a dog sees a rattlesnake or snake in general, they often try to kill it after a predator instinct kicks in. Many ranchers out in my area **use e-collars to train their dogs to leave snakes alone.** Barking from a safe distance is great. Getting bit and dying is not great. There are very specialized classes featured defanged or pretend snakes that use e-collars to teach dogs to steer clear of a snake instead of getting close.

You may or may not have any need for that last part. I have no idea. Maybe you live in the neck of New York City and you're thirty stories up and you live in an urban landscape. There are no snakes for miles around you. You'd have to try hard to go find one. Well, another common example of what you might use an e-collar for is to **prevent your dog from eating that thing he or**

she is not supposed to. You know what I'm talking about. Whether is a piece of chocolate you accidentally drop while cooking or a bug that has no business near your pet, many owners use an e-collar to keep their dog from eating unidentified or unhealthy substances.

WHAT SHOULD I NEVER USE AN E-COLLAR FOR?

Ah, the flip side. Yes, we know that e-collars can be extremely effective and can have very high success rates. Yes, we also have hearts and yes, we also know that we should **not abuse the power of the e-collar.** These things are used for practical purposes. They are *not* for vanity, for image, or anything else like that. It reminds me of that article where a company had mass dog training seminars where they taught pet owners how to responsibly and safely train with e-collars. Sounds great, right? And it was! This class was geared around teaching your dog not to mark things, bark, blah blah blah. The basic sort of things that you want to teach your dogs, and in some cases, the owner of the class said that the power went to the owner's heads.

What do I mean? One example that springs to mind is that of an owner who had not had a lot of success with other training methods, so he signed up for the class and found remarkably good results. All of a sudden, he found that he was able to control his pet and that his dog was now the model of good behavior. The owner, which may have been a guy or a girl, but out of laziness (excuse me, simplicity) I will be using "him" as I have not the slightest idea which gender this person was and I've learned that I should clarify. Anyway, this dude trained dogs for dog shows, right, so he should definitely know better than to abuse any training method, much less an e-collar.

But for this one dog, for whatever reason, the dog just got it. The dog understood and the training was going along wonderfully, which is when the pet owner decided to use the power of the e-collar to do all kinds of other things, like to improve the dog's stance when walking down the aisle. He contacted the owner of the classes to find out how.

Hold on. Just a brief warning here—this is probably going to be a bit of a rant. For all of you responsible pet owners out there, this is not directed at you and I love you. For all you people who do stuff like this, shame on you! That's just unacceptable. A dog can make a connection between "I pee on shoes, I get shocked." A dog can make the connection between "I bark at the neighbor's cat for an eternity and I get shocked." A dog cannot, and I can't stress this enough, make the connection between "my tail needs to be angled more up, or I get shocked." A human might struggle to figure out what was happening. Let me flip this here for a second—if I was over here with an e-collar and every time I put the spoon in the microwave by accident and I'd get a little jolt, it would not take me too long to figure out what was happening. But, if I was just walking around and I'd randomly get a jolt, I'd probably have no idea what in the blue blazes was happening. I wouldn't know that it was whenever I walked with a weird step for whatever. I'd just know I was getting shocked.

And thus, here we come to the crux of the matter: **if your dog cannot reliably understand what's happening, you aren't allowed to use the e-collar.** Really. It's that simple. Used properly, an e-collar can strengthen a dog's training and discipline, keep them from dangerous situations, and teach them not to misbehave. Used improperly, it's just not okay.

Do I Have to Use an E-Collar if I Own It?

This question here is so blatantly obvious to me that I almost regret having to answer it, but here's the fact: sometimes, people buy e-collars and think that it's like they're marrying the collar, that since they have now taken that step, they must carry on with it and never again stray. It's like they're in some 1980s action movie and buying the collar is the equivalent of ordering your squadmates back to the chopper while you stay behind and hold off the enemy—like some dramatic, end-all, forever hold your peace sort of thing. But it isn't. It really, really isn't. **You can own and have an e-collar without using one all the time.**

For all intents and purposes, an e-collar is the same dang thing as a normal collar, except it has an extra function you can use. It's like if you own a truck with four wheel drive. You don't need to have four wheel drive all the time (I'm a Texan. Sorry if my analogies are always redneck) unless you're getting off the beaten path and need to avoid slipping all over the known universe. But, when you need it, it's nice to have. Push a button, and voila, you now have four wheel drive, but for the vast majority of the time, you do just fine with two wheel. Same thing with the e-collar. **Have an e-collar. Use it when you need.** There is no requirement that you must activate your e-collar so many times per month. There isn't a quota. Nobody's counting. Use it all the time or once. Nobody really cares. All that you should care about is that it's not hurting your dog and that it's helping, or at least can be a good backup plan. Of course, like I said before, even if you do this, make sure to rotate it every four hours to make sure that there aren't any rubbing places that will cause your pet discomfort.

For everyone in the back who couldn't hear me say that, I'll say it again. **By buying an e-collar, you are not forced to use it ever.** Heck, you could buy one and literally never turn it on. Why would you do this? I have not the slightest idea, but there's a sort of feeling that if you decide to buy one, you're "resorting" to it and now you're stuck with it. Now that you've decided to buy one, you have to use it. Nope. You are still fully able to carry on training with other things, and hey, maybe your dog is a model of perfect behavior and figures out what you want from 'em every time, except they really, really like to bark when your neighbor Gary waters his plants. Maybe you can't always be around to get him to quit barking at Gary, so you use an e-collar for that and use other kinds of training for everything else. It's not an all-or-nothing sort of situation. No bomb will go off you never even turn it on. Nobody's putting a gun to your head and ordering you to use anything. Use as necessary, at a level that is safe, responsible, and healthy.

Chapter 5. Things to Watch Out For While Using An E-Collar

Things are not all sunshine and rainbows in the e-collar camp. Maybe you're read up to this point and it's looking like everything clear skies and smooth sailing from here on out. You know what to do. You're safe. You're responsible. You're informed. You're determined to do the right thing and get the job dog in a healthy way. Well, first off, great for you and I wish you the best of luck, but there's one, eency-weency, teeny-tiny, insignificant little problem: **You can do everything right and things can still go wrong.**

This is true for everything, of course. You could carefully plan the perfect beach day with your family, book all these wonderful outside activities, make sure you have enough time to get from Point A to Point B, set up everything, pack the proper food, make sure that everyone's got sunscreen, get all the chargers and the picnic basket and the picnic blanket, and halfway through your wonderful sunny beach day, it starts pouring rain and the whole thing's shot. Bummer. It sucks It's unfair. You did everything right and you still ended up failing and having a terrible time. But, as I'm sure you're unfortunately aware, things don't always go according to plan, no matter how careful, thought-out, and researched your plans might be. Same thing goes for e-collars. You can do all the research online, find the best rated collar with all the features you want, make sure it's the right size for your dog, take a training class, blah blah blah, and it can still go badly. And, just like you could stay outside on the beach in the pouring rain, you could just keep soldiering on, but that's probably a terrible idea. Here are a few rainstorms you could encounter on this e-collar quest.

IS YOUR DOG AGGRESSIVE?

This is a no brainer in my opinion, but here goes because it's one of the most important ones for everyone to understand. Sit on the beach in the rain and you get wet. Push an aggressive dog, and you get bit. As a general rule of thumb, **don't use an e-collar if your dog is aggressive.** In an ideal world, all dogs would be friendly and loving towards their owners, but some dogs just aren't. They're mean and scary and kind of intimidating. Sometimes, owners of such dogs try all kinds of methods to get their dog to act the "right way." Maybe the dog get's aggressive when you get after it and scold it. Big warning sign. Big, big warning sign. If your dog reacts very poorly to something like that, they're almost certainly a terrible candidate for an e-collar, even at very low levels. Raise the level, and you may be making the problem even worse.

Aggressive dogs can be extremely dangerous, both to their owners and to the people around them. Do not, and I can't stress this enough, take this lightly—

especially if your dog is a big one that can actually do damage. My aunt had the meanest chihuahua you have ever seen, just a doughy, overweight little canister of hate. She was highly aggressive and mean beyond belief, but she was also the size of a soup can with legs, so her ability to damage anything maxed out at biting people when they weren't looking on the back of their legs. She was irritating, and mean, and vicious, and sort of harmless. I guess, if you picked her up, she might be able to do more damage, but it was no mystery why people started waring just boots when they went to visit my aunt. I would never recommend using an e-collar on her because it was probably backfire in a big way but even in the worse case scenario, she wasn't that dangerous. Maybe some scratches. A tiny nip. That's not to say that her behavior was acceptable or fine, but if your dog is even a little bit dangerous, it isn't okay for them to be highly aggressive. Yes, you probably don't want your dog to be chummy with everyone. If someone broke into my house, I would not want to see my dog getting a belly rub from the robbers. But you get (hopefully) what I'm saying here: **an aggressive dog is a dangerous dog.** If your pet falls into this category, I would *heavily* recommend speaking with a professional, and you would probably be wise to avoid an e-collar.

DOES YOUR DOG HATE REMOTES?

Does your dog break into a rage every time you pick up the TV remote? Probably not. Hopefully not. If it does, you probably have problems. But, for the vast majority of you readers, no, of course your dog doesn't do that. Why? Because your dog has zero reason to hate your TV remote. It has never done anything bad to your pet, and therefore, your pet could care less if you're fiddling with the TV remote.

Was this a lesson about the relationship between dogs and TV remotes? Nope! It's a Segway into my next point: **the three types of e-collars.**

Containment Systems: Containment systems are about as simple as they sound. They're very basic, and the odds are that if you've only heard of one of the three, it's this one. This is the electric fence premise. If your dog crosses the barrier, they get an instant response from the collar. These collars are simple, they don't require a lot from you as an owner, and they're handy for all kinds of folks.

Bark Collars: Most of you dog owners have had that moment where your dog will just not quit barking. It's in no danger, nothing bad or harmful is coming that way, but your dog has decided it will bark endlessly at something for zero reason whatsoever and it's so loud and constant that you're ready to pull your hair out if the neighbors don't give you the boot first. Case in point—I lived in a house with a dresser in the corner, an innocent little dresser that did nothing to nobody. About three weeks after I bought it, one time in the night I guess it gave my bulldog a dirty look and/or he noticed it for the first time, and from that point on, he would never. Stop. Barking. At. It. This kind of collar helps with that sort of activity by administering the stimulus automatically upon a bark.

Obedience Collars: Ah, here's the one that applies. Obedience collars are where things get… tricky. Why? Because they introduce a new factor: you. With Containment System and Bark Collars, you don't have to do much. It's simple and not too much work, but Obedience Collars are a whole different kind of animal because you're in the driver's seat. These aren't activated automatically. You get to activate them as much as you so wish by the handy-dandy remote included.

Why should you care about any of this? What was the weird thing about remotes? Because (ready for this?) **your dog might figure out that the remote is the thing disciplining him and will hate your remote forever.** See, I knew it would come back around! Your dog doesn't give a bit of interest about your TV remote because it has no bearing on its life. But a remote that controls the collar… well, that affects your pet quite a bit. Some dogs might never put two and two together. They might never figure out that when you push the button on the remote, the collar activates.

But if they do… you'll wake up with the destroyed remains of a remote. Here's the thing: dogs can be very smart, and if they decide that the remote is actually the thing causing them discomfort, they aren't going to learn the important lesson. They aren't going to get the lesson you're trying to teach. They aren't going to make progress. They aren't going to get better trained. They aren't going to do anything, because as far as they're concerned, the collar is a little devil that they must destroy. We know how dogs think. If you walk up to your dog today, right now, and whack them (please don't, this is just an example, and you should never do that), they'll wonder what just happened. Do it enough times, and they're pretty quickly hate you. Same thing here. If they don't realize that they're being disciplined for the right thing but in fact decide that the remote is the cause of their problems, not only will your training never work, but it's going to be a real pain in the neck as your dog might be aggressive and hostile towards the remote.

What's the solution? Don't let your dog see the remote. Some people keep it in their back pocket, or in their coat, or somewhere that isn't immediately obvious. Don't just wave it around in front of your pet like "see this? If you chew this thing up, the collar won't work!"

DOES YOUR DOG FUNCTION WITHOUT AN E-COLLAR?

Here's one you may or may not have thought about: **lots of dogs are "collar dependent."** What does that mean? That means, basically, that the dog is extremely well trained and awesome with a collar on, but the moment the collar comes off, all hell breaks loose and the dog becomes a wild mess.

This is a real pain to fix once it's been established, but luckily for us, there's a very easy way to fix it before it even begins! Lucky us! **To avoid this,** the trick is to not let your dog realize that the collar is the source of your training. Don't buy an e-collar and instantly start using it. That's how this mess starts, because then you really haven't taught your dog anything other than how to behave when they collar is on. The moment the collar is off, whoosh, everything's out the window and you're back to square one.

The fix is simple: **get your dog used to the e-collar before ever using it.** No matter how eager you might be to start, hold your horses. Your dog will recognize the e-collar. It feels different than a traditional collar, so get your dog used to it first before ever turning it on. In an ideal world, you're going to want to shoot for a couple weeks of your dog just wearing it. That way, it isn't linked up in your furry friend's brain. Let them get used to the weight of it, the feel, the sensation, so that everyone's normal for them when you begin training with the e-collar. When the dog pairs the idea of the training with the collar itself, it defeats the purpose and the moment you take the collar off, you're no better off than when you started.

CAN YOU SAY, "SHORT TERM?"

Another very common, but very bad, decision is to use the e-collar as a short term solution. To what? To basically anything. Slap some lipstick on a pig and it is still a pig. Slap a collar on a dog to make them behave because your boss is coming over for a BBQ at your house and your dog does unspeakable things to the lower legs of visitors, and you've still got a dog that does unspeakable things to the lower legs of visitors. The problem is still there.

That brings up the vital point of that **there are no quick fixes in dog training, period.** That includes any training method you could imagine and, yes, e-collars fall into that category. This is an especially large problem when a dog is not ready for a certification that's right around the corner. The owner panics, slaps an e-collar on, and doesn't actually teach the dog anything other than to behave short term. But, what's the problem with that? Isn't that okay? Well, no, and here's why: trying to use an e-collar as a short term fix actually causes a lot of long-term problems that are much, much more difficult to sort out than if you just did it properly the first time. It's a process, and one that must be followed.

IS YOUR DOG A NERVOUS ONE?

You have all seen them—sweet dogs that come completely unglued the moment someone raises their voice at them, dogs that get really panicky about the branch rubbing the outside of your house every now and then, dogs that think the world is coming to an end the moment they hear a suspicious sound. My sister's dog is this kind of dog. Lovely little beastie, but my heavens, is he a nervous dog. His latest obsession is the toads outside her apartment. Thanks to the window placement, if he stands in the right place he can just barely see into the backyard, where everything looks completely safe and normal to him, except there's a large population of toads that emerge during the night like a colony of ridiculous vampires. They proceed to sort of mill around in the darkness, causing no harm and doing nothing intimidating, but to my sister's Pomeranian, it's time to buckle down the hatches and go to Red Alert, because these toads are the scariest, most anxiety inducing things that he's ever seen. Unless he is stopped, he will bark for hours at the slightest movement of one of the unsuspecting toads in the dark. Some dogs are just nervous dogs. Things frighten them easily. They're not the bravest of the bunch, and that's fine.

But these nervous dogs come up a lot in e-collar training debates, because one of the common myths is that e-collars are terrible for such beasties. Such dogs can be difficult to train because they are wildly insecure and the strangest things, things that seem to be perfectly safe and not scary to us, can scare the bejeezus out of them. We still care for them, but they're insecure, easily frightened, and prone to be scared, and logically, anything that's insecure, easily frightened, and prone to be scared would not function well with a collar that is capable of giving them electric shocks, right? I mean, if the toads got my sister's dog going that bad, one could only imagine the sort of chaos that would emerge from him using an e-collar. Why, his cute little life would transform into that of fear and terror, right?

Wrong.

Actually, the opposite is true. Despite logic pointing towards the opposite, reality proves otherwise. Many experts actually say that **nervous dogs are some of the best candidates for e-collars.** You have to correctly administer the e-collar training (remember, you can take classes and consult a professional to figure out exactly what to do for your particular dog) but it's a well accepted fact that even your most prone to terror dog excels through e-collar training more than their more aggressive and confident counterparts. Of course, the key still lies on using the e-collar "correctly." Use it badly, and it becomes just another thing that confuses and terrifies them. Use it properly, and they'll probably learn exceedingly quickly.

ARE YOU A LAZY TRAINER?

Hopefully, you answered that question by saying that no, you aren't a lazy trainer and that you want nothing but the best for your dog and you're willing to put in the time and effort to do so. If that's you, we're done here. Give yourself a big pat on the back, skip to the next bit, and maybe even give yourself a gold star because you're what the dog community is all about.

However.

If you're the person that had to kind of think about it, **an e-collar is not for you.** If you just want Fido to quit running out of the fence, maybe you could do it because the user isn't all that important. If you want Fido to stop barking when you're not at home, maybe that would make sense for the same reason. But, and I can't stress this enough, if you're a person that wants a remote activated collar and you are *not* dedicated, you might want to steer clear.

E-collars can be fantastic training tools, but they only work if everyone is on the same page. The dog has to understand. You have to understand. The collar has to do what it's supposed to. That's the only way this works. If even one of those is off, the whole plan is blown and you get to start over from scratch. A big myth is that trainers who use e-collars are lazy, which isn't true no more than saying a trainer who uses treats is lazy. However, it would be plenty fair to say that a lazy trainer who uses an e-collar is lazy. If you activate the collar at random times, the dog will have no idea what's happening and therefore will never learn. If you want to teach your pet to stop chewing on your dress shoes, you can't activate the collar sometimes and sometimes not. It has to be **consistent. Consistency is key.** If every third time you turn on the collar, for your dog, it's like if a random bolt of lightning came out of the sky— completely unpredictable, not from any sort of logical place, and not for punishment. It's just a random bolt of lighting. It's just a random stimulus from the shock collar. It's randomly tripping down the stairs. If it isn't consistent, it's just another random part of your dog's life and the connections won't be drawn. Yes, it's true. To some owners, maybe being able to just push a button sounds like a great plan and it attracts some lazy owners who think it's a miracle pill of the dog training world, but it isn't. It's a tool, and you need to use it properly to have any kind of success.

Of course, we are biologically human and inherently flawed. We can't be around all the time. We have social lives, work. We get distracted. We might not notice things. I'm not saying you have to be a perfect human being and have the eyes of an eagle, but the closer that you get to 100% off the time activating the collar when your dog chews on your dress shoes, the faster and easier the lesson will be.

IS THE SETTING WRONG?

Remember how I said that modern day collars have a bunch of sensitivity levels to precisely land how much you need? Yeah. It's a great feature, and I would never recommend you try anything other than that. The number of levels vary from collar to collar. Some only have a few and others give you the option to fine tune it a lot more.

Your sensitivity setting is potentially the most important thing for an e-collar. This seems like it should be sort of obvious, but some new owners figure that it's all kind of the same thing and as long as you push the button at the right time, you'll be fine. Wrong. Incorrect. Very bad idea. See, it's like if your friend tries to steal a French fry off your plate and you give them a little playful swat to tell them not to. Good. You can do that. You can also whip out an aluminum baseball bat and swing like you're Babe Ruth and you're going to a home run in the ninth inning. Obviously, these are two very different things. One will give your friend an obvious "dang it, those are my fries" and the other will take your friend to the hospital. You bet it's important to distinguish that.

Just to clarify here, no collar has a "send dog to the hospital/vet" option. That's just an example. If it does have that option, get a new collar ASAP. But the point is, your initial collar level is crucial. Nobody here wants to hurt their dog. Nobody here gets all excited about causing discomfort to their dog, and if they do, I ask that you give your dog to someone who will care for it properly because that's just not acceptable in any way, shape or form. But, where do you start with the levels?

Start as low as possible. Yup, it really is that simple. Start with the lowest sensitivity and, if it's too low, work your way up carefully and gradually. Pay attention to how your dog reacts, because that's where you'll get the reading for if you should go up or down. It's recommended that you should put the level somewhere around where your dog notices it, but isn't in pain.

One article that I read pointed to that when you have the right sensitivity, your dog should perk up his or her ears and/or look around and look around as if to say "what was that?" Your dog should not, I repeat, your dog should *not* be in pain. If you're unfamiliar with what to look for, a dog in pain will yelp, react like something hurt it, put its tail between its legs, and so forth. The optimal level is not designed to hurt your pet. It's designed to get its attention and let it know that it did something wrong.

A dog's sensitivity varies enormously. I
remember coming across a story of an owner that had a
Lab. This owner was interested by the concept of e-
collar training since her friend also had a Lab that had
been pretty unruly and resistant to training until the e-
collar came up. Long story short, you guessed it, the
friend talked the owner into giving it a shot. After all,
they had the same kind of dog that was roughly the
same age, so if it worked for the friend's dog, it would
work for her dog, right? The logic is sound enough, but
there was a problem that was almost immediately
revealed: not all dogs are the same, even if they're the
same breed. The owner put an e-collar on her dog and
instead of doing what I just said, about starting as low
as possible and finding the right level, she assumed that
her dog was similar enough to her friend's that she
could use the same sensitivity setting. She was very
wrong, and she was horrified to find that her dog was
apparently quite a bit more sensitive to it and ended up
having to put the sensitivity level much lower. So, the
lesson of this story is that every dog has a unique
sensitivity to the e-collar, and it's in everyone's best
interest to just take your time and find the right setting.

This is a lengthy answer here, but that's because
this is a vital question that you need to take seriously.
Don't worry. We're getting close to everything you
should know about initial levels. I used to think that
saying this last part wasn't necessary but, upon some
more research, I discovered that yes, someone out there

needs to hear this, so here goes. **Find the right level when your dog is doing something wrong.** Don't just randomly press the buttons until it looks like it's the right level and then use it as discipline because it will confuse the blue blazes out of your dog and they will never understand that it's as discipline, not to mention that it's a disciplinary device and shouldn't be used casually. Just throwing that out there for whoever needed to hear that.

Chapter 6. How to Train a Dog Using an E-Collar

Hooray! You made it to the big finale! Well, it isn't a finale, but it is big and it's why a lot of you bought the book in the first place: the hard, down to earth, step by step training. You may or may not have any experience with the actual lessons, and that's fine. You have resources! Also, before we jump in, I want to clarify something here: you can do it. Yes, you. I don't know you, and I have never seen you, but you can. E-collar training is available and usable for basically everyone. You don't need to be a genius. You don't need to be a superhuman. Though it may seem complicated and worrying, it's actually not a scary process whatsoever! The one thing that you're absolutely going to need is some **trust.** If this is a dog that you don't know, spend some time getting their trust or this just won't work.

There are **three basic steps to e-collar training.** First off is the **Introduction phase,** where you basically teach your dog what's happening with the e-collar and what it's all about. Then comes the **Moderate phase,** which is where you and your dog now fully understand what's happening and you can move on to move advanced, difficult things. Then, finally, comes the **Final Phase,** where basically you can fine tweak things as necessary. Through this chapter, I'll be taking you through all of these. If you've read other books or articles or seen videos about these steps, you may recognize them, maybe with different names, but the spirit lives on. Get ready for a long chapter!

WHAT ABOUT THE INTRODUCTION PHASE?

You guessed it! The Introduction Phase is... the first phase! To give you an idea of what we're looking at here, your dog has no idea what an e-collar is. You've never put one on them, and they don't know what in the blazes you're doing.

What you're going to need: you're going to need a dog (duh), yourself (duh), an e-collar, a leash, snacks/petting/treats/some way to make your dog happy, and a **marker word**. This is, depending on your dog, possibly the most fun phase. You don't need much, just patience and dedication.

Marker words are going to be your dog's happy word. Whenever you say it, something good happens, if it's a treat or petting or whatever. Your dog needs to like to hear this word. However, they are also dogs and do not speak your language, so though technically it is a word, it can be anything your heart desires, from a clicker to a simple "yes (common and popular choice)" to a banshee war cry. It doesn't matter, as long as it stays consistent.

Here's how it works: get right in front of your dog, holding a snack they like. Don't be packing around a full turkey because they like turkey. Keep it pretty small, as you'll be doing this quite a bit and you don't want them getting full. Anyway, stand in front of your dog and say your marker word. For our purposes, we'll be using the word "good." "Good!" you shout, and then instantly you give your dog a treat. Note that I say instantly, because your dog needs to know that the marker word is associated with treats. Keep doing this for a while. Many experts say upwards of a dozen or two times is best, so I would recommend doing this somewhere mildly private so your neighbors don't get sick of hearing you yell "good!" For this part, there is **no e-collar.** Your entire goal here is to make sure that Fido understands the connection between your marker word and treats.

Next, you step up your game. The point of this part is to teach your dog to come over to you when they hear the marker word. You're going to **need a leash** for this part, but you aren't at the e-collar yet. How long a leash? Well, that's up to you, but you should look for something at least ten feet long. Much longer than that and you're going to have problems because no matter how much your dog might want to come to you, if they're tripping over a hundred foot leash, it won't work well. Here, you're just going to wait until your dog wanders to the end of the leash, then you're going to tug the leash until they notice it **accompanied with the**

word "come" or however you want to call your dog over, then say your marker word. Your dog should come hauling towards you, and when they arrive, reward them with lavish pets and a treat. Remember how I said that your dog will like this? Yeah. This is why.

Of course, your dog may be a wild one or like mine. Training him was funny, because he'd be full hustling towards me (I'd say sprinting, but he's a bulldog so it was closer to a determined waddle) and get distracted halfway there. No worries. If your dog does this, just give a light leash tug to guide them back. Do this until it's an easy connection, at least a couple dozen times to be sure. Excuse me. At least a couple dozen *good* times. If it fails a couple dozen times, start over.

It's now time for the e-collar.

Yes, it is time. You whip out your handy dandy e-collar, the e-collar that you have been conditioning your dog to and getting him or her used to the feeling of for the past while so it's not an entirely new sensation to him, the e-collar that you already put at just the right level so your dog notices it would hurting it. Yes, that one.

HOW TO WEAR ?

- Place the collar on the pet's neck,adjust the body and buckle it

- The collar should not be too tight. It is best to leave a gap of about 1 inch. It should not be too loose, otherwise it may not work properly.

You put the e-collar on the dog. Duh. But, less duh, make sure it's connecting properly. I'd heartily recommend making sure that nothing's impeding the collar's correct positioning but try to avoid putting the probes on the larynx of your dog (right down the center of the bottom of their throat). A **common mistake here** is attaching the leash to the e-collar, which is a no-no. This is the same exact exercise, except this time, you had added in an e-collar. Don't change anything else.

Next, you're going to wait until your dog's distracted by something. You're going to activate the collar, which, again, is a "what was that" sort of feeling here, not a "auughhhh, my throat" sort of feeling here, say "come", and when they look over, say your marker word and reward them when they get over to you. This is literally the same exercise, except you're using the e-collar in conjunction with your come command. The biggest difference is that you're going to want to keep this **pretty brief—maybe ten minutes.**

Next, comes play time! Have fun with your dog (without an e-collar)! Yay!

You're going to want to keep doing this. Some trainers advise different things you can add in, but that's the basics. One thing I read somewhere that I, personally, think is very important is to just stand there with the e-collar, buzz the e-collar, and give your dog a treat. Don't say anything. The buzz means that Fido is going to get a treat. Don't just keep doing this, but do it every now and then so they realize the e-collar isn't scary and can be, in fact, a delicious and tasty treat.

Speaking of treats, here's something that should be obvious but I'll say it for the people in the back: **for treats to work, your dog must like them.** I know. No matter how tasty Grandma's grilled asparagus is, your dog will not hustle across the lawn for some of Grandma's grilled asparagus. Your dog must actually care about and want to eat whatever treats you have. Just for ease of use, I'd recommend that you just buy a bag of treats, but if you want to do something else, that's fine—just make sure it's something your dog will want. But what if your dog doesn't care about food? They're out there. No worries. Just reward through petting and do the same thing otherwise.

How Long Should I Be in the Introduction Phase? A while. Your dog might be the smartest dog on the planet, but it's still a good idea to wait up to a week. Just don't, under any condition, try and skimp on this. Give it a few days at the minimum, because you won't be getting away with anything. You'll just have to work extra hard later to make up for it, and having solid groundwork is vital.

WHAT ABOUT THE MODERATE PHASE?

Whew! We made it through the first third! That wasn't so hard, was it? Well, I have good and bad news. The good news is that you've completed a third of your phases! The bad news is that if you are going to fail, it's probably going to be here. This can be tricky, because this is when you start adding in other factors. Your dog will be further away, with longer durations, and with a lot more distractions. How can this go bad? Well, if you don't do this right, **your dog will not listen to you if he isn't wearing the e-collar.** You're going to need to make the jump from training using the e-collar to not, and you're going to have to shake a few things up. Ready? Let's go!

There are **four combinations of e-collar use and treats/praise** that you'll be working with here. Again, though it may look scary, with practice and effort, this will not be a big deal.

First off the line comes **E-collar with reward.** This is the one we've been working with for a while now, and basically, you use your command with your handy dandy e-collar and give a treat.

Second comes **e-collar without reward.** Not fundamentally different, but your dog won't like it as much because, you guessed it, no treat. Here, you'll use the e-collar, but the dog won't be getting a treat. Instead, your furry friend will be waiting until you release them from the command.

Next is **no e-collar with reward.** Yay, treats are back! Give the command without your e-collar, but give your dog a treat when they do it.

Finally, we have **no e-collar without reward.** Ah, no treats again. This time, you will just tell your dog a command and they'll just do it without a treat following. Simple as pie. Theoretically.

Now, one obvious question is **what order do you do these in?** Well, here's your answer: it really doesn't matter. Mix it up. Get freaky. Get creative. What you are essentially doing here is making sure that your dog will listen to you with or without a treat and/or an e-collar. You're going to want to do this on all the commands that your dog should by now know well, like "sit," "come," "do my taxes (wait, not that one)" and any others.

Don't rush this. Remember how I said people can get into trouble on this phase and things go wrong? Yeah, it's because people realize that they only have one phase after this and they're all antsy to get going and don't spend enough time here and the whole thing falls apart. How long do you have to be in this phase? Well, how long do you have? Ideally, you're going to want to spend a lot of time in this phase. Add in other factors, like distance, distractions, duration, blah blah blah. Don't change things fundamentally or change things too suddenly and too dramatically, just make minor changes and make sure that your dog gets it and everything's working before moving on. This is not a race.

One thing that a lot of owners find fun is **going for walks.** Wander around with your dog. Teach them have to behave using the four variations above. Many owners use a "structured" walk, meaning that the dog stays with them and doesn't sniff around, pee on stuff, poop, blah blah blah until they get a release command do what they want. Now, a brief word of warning: your dog must be ready for this. This is obvious, but **if your dog ignores you while on the leash, now is not the right time to let him off the leash.** Even if your dog is a wonder dog and everything smooth sailing, don't think nothing can go wrong. These are still living creatures, after all, that that will always throw in a degree of uncertainty. Have a backup plan in case something does go wrong.

The name of the game here in the 2nd phase, just like the first one, is practice, practice, practice.

WHAT ABOUT THE FINAL PHASE?

Woohoo! We made it to the last phase! Didn't I tell you that you could do it? E-collar training has this giant fear around it, and yet, that wasn't so hard at all, now was it? Maybe it took some time and effort, but that's true for any kind of training.

But, wait, you say. What could possibly happen in this last phase? Everything's already been done. You've worked with your dog endlessly, taught them everything, stuck it out when your patience was potentially worn thin, and you've practiced, practiced, practiced. Here's the good news, and why this phase seems suspiciously short compared to the last two: **the work's done.** Nothing new here changes. You aren't adding anything new, as you should have already done that in the Moderate phase.

Here's how to know if you're actually ready to be in the Final Phase:

Your dog is reliable off the leash. A huge one. If your dog, the moment you remove the leash, flies off into the middle distance to catch that squirrel, you need more work. If your dog remembers his or her training and always does what you say, great!

Your dog responds to your commands. This one explains itself, but if your dog doesn't listen to you all the time, you're going to need more work.

Your dog understands your e-collar and does not fear it. Your dog should not be afraid of it. Your dog should trust you. If this is not true, you need to do a lot of work to repair that bond.

ARE YOU READY FOR YOUR POP QUIZ?

Pop quiz time! Yes, please put all electronic gadgets away, take out a single sheet of paper and a pencil, and get ready for your pop quiz! Here's the only question: **is your dog perfect?**

Think about it. Answer it. Write it on the piece of paper. Pencils down!

If the answer on your piece of paper is anything but no, e-collars might be a bad choice for you. My dog is perfect in my mind. He's adorable and sweet and lovable and funny. But, in a much more literal way, he's not perfect. He's very well trained, but I can never and should never assume that he will behave perfectly under all conditions. **No dog, no matter how well trained, can be reliable every single time.** Nine thousand, nine hundred and ninety nine times in a row, your dog may be a perfect angel, but maybe something weird happens that last time. If I had to impart one piece of advice in this whole book to you, it would be this: **BE PREPARED IN CASE SOMETHING HAPPENS THAT YOU AREN'T EXPECTING.** It's just not worth risking, when your dog's life or something else's life could depend on you being prepared for the "what if" situations. E-collars are fantastic, but they are not a fix all. You need to be prepared, even if you are a skilled trainer and your dog is will trained and has good manners.

Chapter 7. Common Questions and Answers

You've theoretically read through this little book and, maybe, you still have questions. I will try to have answers for you. Now, this is going to be a little tricky, seeing as you and I have never met and there's no conceivable way for me to know what you might ask, but here's a few things that I think you might be curious about that weren't defined much in other parts of the book. Good? Good.

Is E-Collar Training Hard?

No, it is not. E-collar training can be much easier than other styles of training, depending on your dog and you yourself. E-collar training is designed to be efficient and accessible. Anyone who is a responsible dog owner, half a brain, some patience, and a love for their dog can do it. Some dogs will take longer than others. That's just nature and basically the luck of the draw. Some dogs will take forever to train. Others will get it in no time, even in the same breed. But, overall, e-collar training is no more difficult than many other types of training, and, like I said before, it can provide excellent results when performed correctly.

Can I Just Use an E-Collar?

In other words, can you use just an e-collar without any other kinds of training? **Yes, but it's not a good idea.** E-collars work best when combined with things like treats. I read in one source that the E-collar should never be how you train a dog. You train a dog with motivation. An e-collar is just one way to help with motivation, but using it alone isn't nearly as effective or fun for either party as it is with treats and other measures mixed in, as I explained in the chapter before.

What If Stuff Goes Bad?

Theoretically, though these cases are not necessarily common, a dog will just not react properly to an e-collar. Maybe they hate it. Maybe it scares them or freaks them out. Maybe it changes their personality when they feel it. There are a thousand maybes, many of which I've covered in various parts of the book, but no matter what, if it isn't going to way it's supposed to, **consult a professional.** I've said it before and I'll say it again: professionals are your friend, and people who get into dog training care about dogs and know what they're talking about. They will want to help you, and if something seems wrong, don't ignore your gut. Find out how to solve it. Of course, there may be setbacks. Your dog might not understand sometimes what's expected, or you might get the wrong treats. Those are learning curves. But if something actually feels wrong, don't push through. This should not be a bad experience. It should be healthy and positive and effective.

WHAT IF I CAN'T AFFORD A NAME BRAND COLLAR?

I can't stress this enough. **Buy a good collar.** Going name brand is by far the only way to go on this. Do your research, find out what you need, and if you can't afford one right now, don't sweat it. Maybe rent's coming up, you've got car payments, and you really can't afford justifying a higher priced collar when there's something that might work just as well. Don't scrimp. The potential drawbacks of a bad collar is not anywhere near worth it. Just save up and buy one, or go to your local pet store and see if renting is an option. Don't, I repeat, don't cheap out because it can and will cost you later.

IS MY DOG A GOOD FIT FOR AN E-COLLAR?

Honestly? I have not the slightest idea, and neither do you. Various temperaments can be surprising. Remember how I said nervous dogs can perform better than other dogs? Well, that doesn't make any sense, right, but here we are. Dogs respond in very individual ways to an e-collar, and though I could sit here and rant on and on about personality types and breeds, the **only real way to know if your dog is a**

good candidate is to try. Of course, beforehand, you need to vet your dog for a number of things, like if they're old and big enough for it yet to be safe.

Why Can't I Use My Grandpa's Hunting E-Collar?

Older collars are less reliable than modern ones, and they come with a lot fewer features. One of the biggest differences between an ancient collar and a modern day one is the sensitivity controls, which is huge. Old collars were initially made for hunting dogs, and thus, they were designed for a very different purpose. If your dog has a nasty habit of attacking a boar and getting badly injured, yes, you want the shock to be both large and probably painful to get your dog well away from the gigantic, dangerous animal before your dog is badly injured (at least, that was the logic). But alas, these collars I cannot in good conscious recommend, as they tend to be a lot stronger, more volatile, and who knows what might have gone wrong while they've been waiting in the garage for the past thirty years. It's a safety concern. I'm not working for any e-collar companies or anything. I could care less which one you buy, but make sure it's the right one and make sure you're being safe.

Is E-Collar Training Expensive?

Another impossible question for me to answer, but in short, **no.** E-collar training is time consuming, but as far as just eating through your wallet, you don't have much to worry about. The biggest purchase, by far, is the collar itself. You're also going to need some treats, which are very inexpensive, a lot of patience (which is true for any training), and maybe a class if you feel more comfortable with e-collars are taking a training course on it. Overall, though, no. The only larger purchase you're going to need to make is right off the bat, and a good collar should last a long time. They're meant to stick around.

Will People Hate Me?

Remember earlier, when I was talking about if your dog would hate you if you used an e-collar? Yeah? Okay, well, now here's a different but very important question: will your fellow humans hate you? Remember, there is a lot of stigma, myths, and bad images associated with e-collar training, and I do mean a lot. Are these people going to judge you for using an e-collar? Maybe. And who cares? You aren't doing anything for them. If you're an informed dog owner and you decide not to use an e-collar, good for you. If you're an informed dog owner and you decide to use an e-collar, good for you. The key thing is that you do the best you can for your dog with the facts and not a bunch of paranoia and fear based myths. This might upset some people, but I'll be honest with you: **nobody else matters when you're training your dog**, because they aren't the ones responsible if the training is done poorly and if something bad happens. I know someone who cooks a three course meal, lays on the floor, and feed his dogs from a golden spoon three times a day (I'm not kidding). This individual certainly would agree that e-collar training is horrible, but his dog is wild and unruly and owns the house. Does this make this person bad or mean or cruel? No, of course not. It's just different ideologies. We're all in this together. We all want the best for our dogs, but sometimes, fear and bad information get in the way, and it just so happens that such a sensitive subject about something we dog owners all care about can lead to arguments.

CHAPTER 8. CONCLUSION

Well, everyone, the time is coming. The end of the book is nigh. We've had a good time here, or at least I have while writing this. I'm going to miss ya'll. But, luckily, we don't have to go yet! We've gone over a lot of the biggest things that you need to know for e-collar training. You're prepared to train your dog with an e-collar, or at least, you are well informed about the pros, cons, and tactics around them as a whole. Maybe you came in here wanting to learn about e-collars with the intent to use one someday. Maybe you wanted to play devil's advocate and learn about the other side and you're against e-collars. Maybe you're just curious. Whatever the reason is, you found yourself here somehow and I hope you learned a little something here.

You can absolutely do this. There is no doubt in my mind that you are capable of training a dog using an e-collar if you decide to. Despite what many of the fear mongrels might insist based on outdated information and assumptions, a modern e-collar is a healthy tool that can strengthen the bond of a dog and owner, can teach a dog in a healthy and responsible way, and can otherwise improve the dog training community. When handled incorrectly, any form of training can be abused.

I wish you the best of luck in your dog training journey.

WHEN YOU REALIZE YOU WERE THE GOOD DOG ALL ALONG

About The Author

Jack E. Garretson is a dog safety & lyfestile expert, animal advocate and educator. He is passionate about animal studies of all sorts, and Jack is a professional member of some among the most regarded international association of animal behavior and human-animal interaction. He is involved in several projects globally, about animal behavior, animal cognition, education, animal rescue and compassionate conservation. Jack learnt from the best dog trainers from around the world in the videos, and from his experiences at the Canine College, at seminars, and as a dog trainer, he realized the full potential of what you can achieve.

If you've ever had any issues training your dog – Jack is here to serve you as well. If you want to create your perfect pup using a real game-based approach that works – you're in the right place. If you want to create your dream dog without punishing your dog left and right – welcome in.